SPOTLIGHT ON OUR FUTURE

THE FUTURE OF OUR EDUCATION

JANARI AUDRA

NEW YORK

Published in 2022 by The Rosen Publishing Group, Inc.
29 East 21st Street, New York, NY 10010

Copyright © 2022 by The Rosen Publishing Group, Inc.

All rights reserved. No part of this book may be reproduced in any form without permission in writing from the publisher, except by a reviewer.

First Edition

Editor: Theresa Emminizer
Book Design: Michael Flynn

Photo Credits: Cover PeopleImages/E+/Getty Images; (series background) jessicahyde/Shutterstock.com; p. 4 Klaus Vedfelt/DigitalVision/Getty Images; p. 5 https://commons.wikimedia.org/wiki/File:Eleanor_Roosevelt_UDHR.jpg; p. 6 Darryl Brooks/Shutterstock.com; p. 7 Bettmann/Getty Images; p. 9 Fotosearch/Archive Photos/Getty Images; p. 10 littlenySTOCK/Shutterstock.com; p. 11 Dietmar/Temps/Shutterstock.com; p. 13 anasalhajj/Shutterstock.com; p. 14 https://en.wikipedia.org/wiki/George_W._Bush#/media/File:George-W-Bush.jpeg; p. 15 https://en.wikipedia.org/wiki/Every_Student_Succeeds_Act#/media/File:President_Barack_Obama_signs_Every_Student_Succeeds_Act_(ESSA).jpg; pp. 16, 21, 28 Monkey Business Images/Shutterstock.com; p. 17 SOMKKU/Shutterstock.com; p. 19 (miners) Tom Stoddart/Getty Images; p. 19 (coltan ore) Nada B/Shutterstock.com; p. 23 Marla Aufmuth/Getty Images; p. 24 David Grossman/Alamy Stock Photo; p. 25 Katarzyna Uroda/Shutterstock.com; p. 27 JP Yim/Stringer/Getty Images; p. 28 Billion Photos/Shutterstock.com.

Cataloging-in-Publication Data

Names: Audra, Janari.
Title: The future of our education / Janari Audra.
Description: New York : PowerKids Press, 2022. | Series: Spotlight on our future | Includes glossary and index.
Identifiers: ISBN 9781725324046 (pbk.) | ISBN 9781725324077 (library bound) | ISBN 9781725324053 (6 pack)
Subjects: LCSH: Education--Juvenile literature. | Educational change--Juvenile literature. | Education--Curricula--Juvenile literature.
Classification: LCC LB1556.A937 2022 | DDC 370--dc23

Manufactured in the United States of America

Some of the images in this book illustrate individuals who are models. The depictions do not imply actual situations or events.

CPSIA Compliance Information: Batch #CSPK22. For further information contact Rosen Publishing, New York, New York at 1-800-237-9932.

CONTENTS

THE RIGHT TO EDUCATION 4

PUBLIC EDUCATION 6

EDUCATED CHOICES 8

NOT EQUAL FOR ALL 10

GLOBAL EDUCATION 12

ELEMENTARY AND SECONDARY EDUCATION ACT 14

ISSUES IN U.S. EDUCATION 16

LEARNING WITH TECHNOLOGY 18

THE VALUE OF EDUCATION 20

MALALA YOUSAFZAI 22

PROTEST FOR CHANGE 24

YOU CAN HELP 26

IDEAS FOR CHANGE 28

STAYING INFORMED AND INVOLVED 30

GLOSSARY 31

INDEX 32

PRIMARY SOURCE LIST 32

WEBSITES 32

CHAPTER ONE

THE RIGHT TO EDUCATION

A good education is helpful to people all around the world. Education can help people learn about history and their place in the world. It can teach people how to question systems that are in place and create answers to the problems they face. Education can give people the skills they need to better their situation or lifestyle. Educated people are more likely to get jobs and earn more money.

First Lady Eleanor Roosevelt helped create the Universal Declaration of Human Rights.

The United Nations (UN) considers education a basic human right. In 1948, the UN issued the Universal Declaration of Human Rights. It says, "Everyone has the right to education."

Sadly, education isn't always available to people. About 264 million children around the world don't have **access** to quality education. Many groups and people are working to solve this problem. This includes many caring kids!

CHAPTER TWO
PUBLIC EDUCATION

When Europeans first came to North America, they created their own education system. They wanted children to learn to read and write so that they could study the Bible. In 1635, the Boston Latin School became the first public school in the United States. In 1837, people created the first state board of education, which was in Massachusetts. Its goal was to create a structure, or set of rules, for schools to follow.

These bricks mark the spot of the original Boston Latin School.

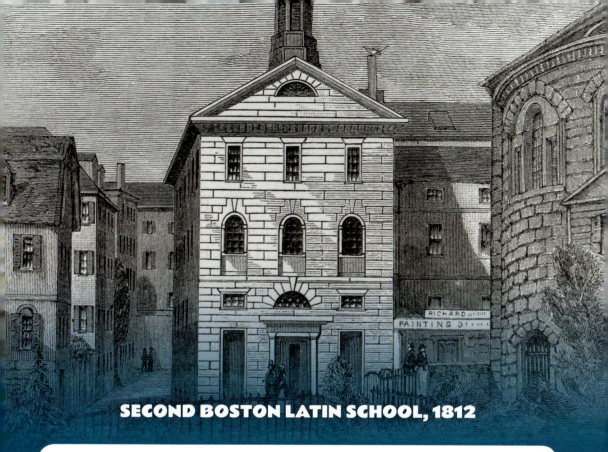

SECOND BOSTON LATIN SCHOOL, 1812

This system wasn't always used. At times, many children couldn't go to school. Instead, they worked on farms or had jobs. Governments created laws protecting child workers during the 19th century.

Today, many countries offer free public education for children. Children are required to attend public schools and learn a standard **curriculum** that teaches basic knowledge and skills. When completing school, students earn a **diploma**.

CHAPTER THREE
EDUCATED CHOICES

The American dream is the idea that any citizen can do well if they work hard enough. Horace Mann was an educator who believed that having a good education makes all people equal. Mann was the first education secretary in the state of Massachusetts. He felt that a good education could help people succeed even if they didn't have the same advantages starting out.

Educated people know more about what's happening in the world. They also have skills that can help them make better choices in life. Educated people are less likely to smoke or drink alcohol. They can also afford to eat healthier foods and are more likely to see a doctor. This helps them lead healthier lives. Putting money toward education reduces, or lessens, poverty and helps create long-term health benefits for people.

Horace Mann worked to improve the education system. He was the first education secretary of Massachusetts.

CHAPTER FOUR

NOT EQUAL FOR ALL

Not every child around the world gets a good basic education. Not everyone has equal money and supplies. Some people have a lot of money while others have very little. This creates a lack of opportunity in some places.

In 2017, the global average income was $15,469. That year the average person living in Qatar made $116,936, while someone living in the Central African Republic made only $661.

This is a school in Malawi. Schools around the world can look very different from one another.

Poverty has a big impact on education. People with less money need to worry about getting food, clothing, and shelter. In the United States, one in seven children lives with hunger. Hunger makes it harder to learn. Poverty also creates stress, or worry, which can make it hard to complete homework or focus on schoolwork. This makes it more likely that children will drop out of school.

CHAPTER FIVE

GLOBAL EDUCATION

There are many reasons why education isn't equal around the world. Sometimes conflict and war make it unsafe to go to school. Syria has been in a civil war since 2011. Because of this, 7,000 Syrian schools have been ruined and about 2 million Syrian children can't attend school.

In some parts of the world, there aren't enough schools for everyone. In other areas, schools are too far away for kids to get to. Some people don't have enough money to send their children to school. Some places don't have enough money to pay for a teacher. Other schools don't have electricity or running water.

In some areas, **technology** is helping education. In Beijing, China, when students can't get to school, they can learn on smart devices such as phones and computers in their homes.

Sometimes children can't make it to school because of unsafe surroundings. These students in Yemen are studying in a house.

CHAPTER SIX

ELEMENTARY AND SECONDARY EDUCATION ACT

Public school in the United States has changed over the years. The Elementary and Secondary Education Act (ESEA) was signed in 1965. This gave government money to school districts with more low-income students. It was meant to help improve education in poor areas.

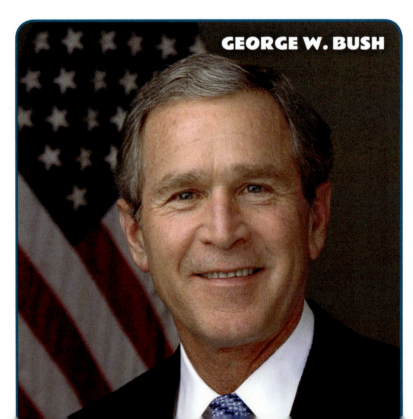

GEORGE W. BUSH

In December 2015, President Barack Obama signed ESSA into law.

The ESEA act has changed a lot. In 2001, President George W. Bush renamed it No Child Left Behind. Many people didn't like the new act. There was a lot of focus on **standardized** testing. In 2015, the law was changed again. It became the Every Student Succeeds Act (ESSA) and focused more on students' **academic** growth.

State and local governments also make many decisions about education. This means things can be very different in different places around the country. School districts with more money often have better schools.

15

CHAPTER SEVEN

ISSUES IN U.S. EDUCATION

The United States has a large public school system. All students can get a free education from kindergarten to the 12th grade. However, there are issues with the U.S. education system. Not all schools are equal. Sometimes, there aren't enough teachers from different backgrounds. The voices of women, black people, and others are often left out of history books. Their stories aren't told as much.

People learn in different ways. Some people believe that standardized testing isn't fair to all students.

There are also some issues with standardized testing. Some people believe these tests only teach students to memorize. Tests may not give a fair picture of the students taking them. They may not show what the student can do or how well the student can learn.

There are also concerns that students spend too much time sitting in school. There's not as much time to explore and play as there used to be.

CHAPTER EIGHT
LEARNING WITH TECHNOLOGY

New technology is changing quickly. It can be used to aid learning and benefit many people worldwide. New computer programs called adaptive learning software are helping teachers work with students as they learn. Teachers can see how much a student understands as they work. Technology isn't meant to replace teachers, but it can help teachers do their jobs better. It can also help students learn in new ways.

However, technology costs money. That means it's less likely to be used in areas that don't have as much money for education, even though those areas may need it more.

Also, the **materials** needed to create these technologies can be harmful to the planet. Computer screens and smart devices contain materials that people dig up from deep within the earth. Mining work is very dangerous and is often done by children.

COLTAN ORE

The kids shown here are mining for coltan. Coltan is a material that's used to make many electronics.

CHAPTER NINE

THE VALUE OF EDUCATION

Societies must decide on what they think students should get from an education. Some people think an education should just prepare students for work. Specialized training and **apprenticeships** can teach people skills such as carpentry so they can work in a particular field.

However, education is more than just learning skills. A broad education helps people understand the world around them. With access to more information, or facts, people are able to make better choices in life. Educated people are also better able to understand how their government works. This helps to keep things fair and keep government officials responsible.

A good education makes people better able to think about important issues. In some countries, the government controls the flow of information. Newspapers can't print the truth, and people can't speak out against unfair laws.

Learning how to become a good citizen is an important part of education.

CHAPTER TEN

MALALA YOUSAFZAI

In some places, people have to fight for access to education. In 2012, a 15-year-old Pakistani girl named Malala Yousafzai spoke up for the right for girls to get an education. A group called the **Taliban** was trying to keep girls from going to school in the area.

Malala wrote a blog called *Diary of a Pakistani Schoolgirl*. She also spoke about the issue on Pakistani television. She became well known. One day, two men from the Taliban stopped Malala's school bus. They shot her.

Malala was badly hurt, but she lived. She was moved to a hospital in Great Britain to heal. Nine months later, she spoke to others at the United Nations in New York. In 2014, when she was 17, she became the youngest person to receive the Nobel Peace Prize.

Malala still speaks out about education around the world. Her newest book, *We Are Displaced*, was published in 2019.

CHAPTER ELEVEN

PROTEST FOR CHANGE

Some young people are working to improve education within the United States. On November 18, 2019, many students in New York City held a protest for educational equality. A student-led group called Teens Take Charge organized the protest.

New York City is very **ethnically** mixed, but many schools are very **segregated**. The city's best high schools have a low percentage of African American and Latinx students, even though there are many students from those groups in the school system. Students from Teens Take Charge wanted the city to make changes to make things more fair. When changes didn't happen, they started protesting.

Students around the world can create change by protesting and speaking up.

   Protesting is one way kids can work for change. Every student in the United States has the right to free speech and the right to have their voice be heard. The power to create a better future is in your hands.

CHAPTER TWELVE
YOU CAN HELP

Young **activists** have proved that their voices can make a difference. It's possible to work for better education for yourself and others.

You can help. You can start right where you live with your family and friends. Literacy, or the ability to read and write, is a growing concern across the United States and the world. Only 37 percent of high school graduates can read at or above their grade level.

Here are some ways you can help people in your community and support literacy:

- Get a library card. This will allow you to borrow books and helps support the library.
- Raise money to give supplies to classrooms in need.
- Volunteer for your local reading group—or help create one.
- Create a book club.
- Collect books for school libraries.

Young activist Amanda Gorman founded One Pen One Page, a group that offers free writing programs to kids in need.

CHAPTER THIRTEEN

IDEAS FOR CHANGE

When working for better education, it's important to set goals. This can help make your efforts more successful. Studying how other education systems work can be helpful. Then you can decide what you think works the best.

In Finland, there's only one standardized test, and students can choose whether to take it or not. In the Netherlands, students have a choice of different types of schools after grade school. Some schools start and stop at different times.

In some countries, students wear **uniforms** to school. Do you think uniforms are a good idea?

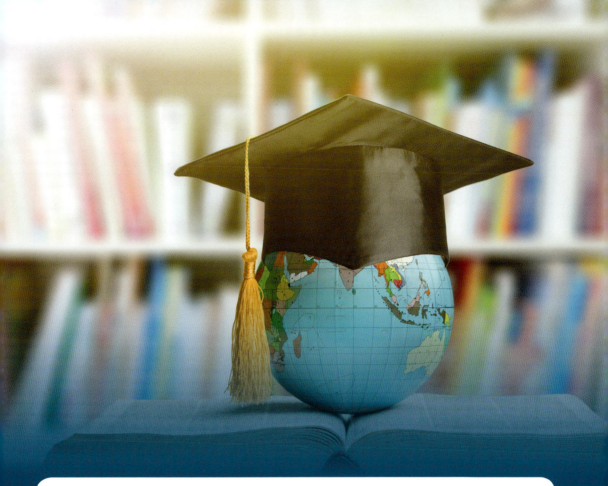

Here are some ways you can help improve education at home and elsewhere:

- Write a letter to your local newspaper.
- Write a letter to a government leader.
- Talk with other students.
- Become a tutor, or someone who helps teach others.
- Start a petition. A petition is a written appeal for something.

CHAPTER FOURTEEN

STAYING INFORMED AND INVOLVED

Education is a basic human right. Unfortunately, education systems aren't always fair. Areas with more money tend to have better schools. In many places, schools are still segregated.

The outbreak of the COVID-19 pandemic in December 2019 demonstrated the importance of health education. Groups such as the CDC and WHO worked to spread awareness about the disease. They urged people to wear masks and social distance in public. Schools across the country worked to educate people about COVID-19 and to keep students safe.

There are many ways that you can help. Collecting books and school supplies to send to schools in need is a good way to start. Learning about different education systems around the world is useful too. As the world changes, so will education. The time to act is now!

GLOSSARY

academic (aa-kuh-DEH-mik) Connected with a school, especially a college or university.

access (AK-sehs) The ability to use or enter something.

activist (AK-tih-vist) Someone who acts strongly in support of or against an issue.

apprenticeship (uh-PREN-tuhs-ship) A period in which a young person works with an experienced person to learn a skill or trade.

curriculum (cuh-RIH-kyuh-luhm) All the courses of study offered by a school.

diploma (duh-PLOH-muh) A document saying that a student has reached a certain standard of education.

ethnically (ETH-nih-klee) Having to do with a group of people who share the same language or the same beliefs, practices, and arts.

material (muh-TEER-ee-ul) Something from which something else can be made.

segregated (SEH-gri-gay-tuhd) Set apart or separated from others, especially because of race.

standardized (STAN-duhr-dizd) Brought into conformity with a standard way.

Taliban (TA-lih-ban) A fundamentalist Islamic militia in Afghanistan.

technology (tek-NAH-luh-jee) A method that uses science to solve problems and the tools used to solve those problems.

INDEX

B
Boston Latin School, 6, 7
Bush, George W., 14, 15

C
Central African Republic, 10
China, 12

E
Elementary and Secondary
    Education Act (ESEA),
    14, 15
Every Student Succeeds Act
    (ESSA), 15

F
Finland, 28

G
Gorman, Amanda, 27
Great Britain, 22

M
Malawi, 11
Mann, Horace, 8
Massachusetts, 6, 8

N
Netherlands, 28
Nobel Peace Prize, 22
No Child Left Behind, 15

O
Obama, Barack, 15
One Pen One Page, 27

Q
Qatar, 10

R
Roosevelt, Eleanor, 5

S
standardized testing, 15, 17,
    28
Syria, 12

T
Taliban, 22
Teens Take Charge, 24

U
United Nations (UN), 5, 22
United States, 6, 11, 14, 16,
    24, 25, 26
Universal Declaration of
    Human Rights, 5

Y
Yemen, 12
Yousafzai, Malala, 22

PRIMARY SOURCE LIST

Page 5
Eleanor Roosevelt holding poster of the Universal Declaration of Human Rights. Photograph. Lake Success, New York. November 1949. Obtained through Wikimedia Commons.

Page 7
The Old Latin School illustration. Sketch. Boston, Massachusetts. 1900. Held by Getty Images.

Page 9
Horace Mann. Photograph. Taken before 1859. Held by Getty Images.

WEBSITES

Due to the changing nature of Internet links, PowerKids Press has developed an online list of websites related to the subject of this book. This site is updated regularly. Please use this link to access the list: www.powerkidslinks.com/SOOF/education